APOSTLE DR. ELIZABETH PEDRO

A Woman in her WAR ROOM
Volume 2

Breaking Through Silence In Marriage

A WOMAN IN HER WAR ROOM
Breaking through Silence in Marriage

Copyright © July 2023
Dr. ELIZABETH PEDRO/KMHP
ISBN Paperback: 978-1-63732-493-6

Produced and Published by:
KINGDOM MEDIA HOUSE PUBLISHING
KINGDOM MEDIA HOUSE
Tel: +8617880217320/+237672645275
Whatsapp: +8617880217320
Email: KMHP_2023@protonmail.com

All rights reserved. No part of this publication should be copied, stored, reprinted for commercial use or gain, or stored in any electronic form without the author's permission, except for brief excerpts in magazines, articles, reviews, etc. For further information or permission, contact the publishers.

To order copies of this book, contact the author via the following contact information:
Telephone/Whatsapp: +1 (780) 999-4183 /+1 (780) 707-6078/ +234 907 114 7565
Email: Elizabethpedro@rocketmail.com
elizabeth@serenitycoachingservies.ca
Facebook: lizyoliha.pedro
Instagram: iamlizpedro
https://SerenityCoachingServices.ca
https://womenhelpingwomenfoundation.com

RECOMMENDATIONS

What an amazing book! In fact, it is also a good manual for dealing with the institution of Marriage as God intended it to be, as well as a useful tool in marriage counseling.

Marriages fail in the secular world and, unfortunately, even in the church because many people want to take "Marriage" designed by God but execute it their way, leading to failures and mishaps.

This book can help you see what you need to start doing, what you may be already doing but need to do more, and what not to do in your marriage.

It must be noted that in spite of the title, it is a must-read for both men and women because the information contained in the book is beneficial to both men and women. I would also recommend it as a very powerful "pre-marriage" self-help guidebook for those planning to marry.

For anyone who the failure of marriage has already hurt, I recommend this book as part of your healing process, helping you understand what could have gone wrong, and helping to encourage you to try again, however, but with more preparation this time.

Her Excellency Rev. Dr. Bokwey Burnley. CDKA

This Five chapter book by Apostle Dr. Elizabeth Pedro is a must-have for every woman as it talks about the woman and her role in a family. Whether married or single, this book will teach you how to understand your role as a woman.

In Chapter One of this book, Apostle Elizabeth gives a detailed description of marriage as God's plan for creation and helps women understand their role and function as wives and mothers. To summarize the woman's role, she cares for herself and caters to the needs of her husband, children, and others in the family. She ends this chapter beautifully by discussing God's blueprint for a successful marriage, as seen in Ephesians 5:18-33, which can be summed as submitting to God and each other.

In Chapter Two of the book, Apostle Elizabeth takes us on a journey of marriage, and she lets the woman know she is a need in the husband's life and her role is crucial, as she can make or break the man and the marriage. The role of the woman as a helper and encourager to her husband and a mother to her children is further explained. I believe every woman reading this chapter will never doubt how important her role as a wife and mother is.

Chapter Three happens to be one of my favorite chapters as the author tells stories of different women to help you connect with her message of the woman and her war room. She shares that many people get married and do not know the battles faced to keep the marriage and family.

She shares the story of Hannah in the Bible, Cecilia Wairimu, Veronica, and others who faced different issues of barrenness, gender inequality, and abuse of various kinds. This chapter is an eye-opener and will make every woman know that they need other women and supportive men to do life better. So dear woman, do not stay silent in your pain. This chapter is personal to Apostle Elizabeth. I can now understand why she has the Women Helping Women for a Sustainable Tomorrow organization, where she and other women are educating and empowering women globally to become better and contribute meaningfully to the community.

Chapter four is another favorite chapter as Apostle Elizabeth teaches how to win the battles a woman faces in the family. She gives tips on strategies to help you win the battles. I will intentionally keep the lessons I learned here to myself as I want you to read this inspiring book to learn the lessons and encourage other women to buy and learn too.

Chapter five concludes this inspirational book, A Woman In Her War Room Volume 2, by giving more tips on how women can intentionally build a better society through all she does in her family and community. She advises women to work as a team with their spouses to create a better society, as their family reflects the larger community. I love the intentionality in this chapter, and as a marriage and family coach that encourages teamwork in the family, I wholeheartedly support teamwork.

I will conclude by saying that this book will make you see tips that are divinely inspired to give you solutions, no matter what you face.

Dear woman or man reading this book, you can win every battle you face as you gain knowledge and fight with the tips Apostle Elizabeth has shared in this powerful book.

Tunde Elesin
Marriage and family counselor
Lead Coach - Character Academy

A WOMAN IN HER WAR ROOM Vol. 2 By Dr. Elizabeth Pedro. The Bible says, "My people are destroyed for lack of knowledge" (Hosea 4:6). But it also says that through knowledge shall the just be delivered (Prov. 11:9).

Dr. Pedro, in this book, provided firsthand and practical knowledge to help women navigate the challenges that today's families face and how to overcome them as VICTORS and not Victims.

I therefore highly recommend this book to all parents and potential parents in this twenty-first century.

H.E. RT HON DR PHILLIP S PHINN, OEA, DCPC
Chancellor of CICA International University

DEDICATION

In our society today, many women are going through numerous things in their marriages and fear speaking out because of fear and societal rejection. This book is dedicated to such women worldwide to strengthen and empower them to break the silence.

I also want to dedicate this book to my sister, Gladys, who died in silence from domestic abuse and damages. She kept her sufferings to herself and couldn't find a way to tell anyone what was happening in her marriage.

Above all, I dedicate this book to God Almighty for the inspiration and strength to join hands with this woman to fight against silence in marriages and relationships. To God be all the glory. AMEN.

ACKNOWLEDGMENT

I thank God Almighty for the grace to put together this Second Edition of "A Woman in Her War Room" despite all the hurdles encountered throughout the process. To Him alone, I give all the glory. Writing this second edition as a follow-up to the first edition is a dream come true. I pray you are blessed as you read.

My special and heartfelt thanks and appreciation also goes to my loving, caring, and supportive husband, His Excellency Ambassador Rev. Shadrach Omokhas, for his encouragement during this journey. Thank you for being so willing to provide the needed support throughout.

To my children, Martin and George Pedro, thank you so much for being my "Why" and "How" and for allowing me time away from you to research and write. Without you both, all the wealth in the world means nothing to me.

To every leader and member of Women Helping Women for a Sustainable Tomorrow (WHW), I want to say thank you for your love, support, and constant prayers for me. May God bless you all and continue to increase the organization towards achieving the vision He has given me.

I also extend my heartfelt thanks to members of Great Shepherd Ministries (GSM) Edmonton members.

Agape Women Ministries Canada and Nigeria, thank you for your prayers and support.

Finally, I want to thank the buyers of this book because you are the inspiration and reason why we invested time and money to produce this book.

TABLE OF CONTENTS

Recommendations	3
Dedication	9
Acknowledgment	10
Table of Contents	13
Foreword	15
Introduction	17
CHAPTER 1	21
UNDERSTANDING THE FAMILY	
• Origin of Family	
• What is Marriage?	
CHAPTER 2	35
THE WOMAN IN HER MARRIAGE	
The Role of the Woman in Marriage	
• As a Wife	
• As a Mother.	
CHAPTER 3	47
SILENT MOMENTS OF THE WOMAN IN HER MARRIAGE.	
• Story 1	
• Story 2	
• Story 3	
CHAPTER 4	65
FIGHTING SILENT BATTLES IN YOUR HOME	
• Caused by your Husband	
• Caused By Your Children	
• Caused by Your In-laws	
• Caused By Yourself	
CHAPTER 5	89
THE IMPORTANCE OF FAMILY TO OUR PRESENT-DAY SOCIETY	

- Our Society Today
- The Importance of Having a Healthy Family to the Society.

Other Books by the Author	99
Women Empowerment Conference Pictures	100
Author's Biography	103
Notes	107

FOREWORD

Marriage and Family have remained God's pertinent institution in advancing the gospel. Women are God's resourceful instrument and weapon of sustainability for continuous marriage and family. Apostle Dr. Elizabeth Pedro has broken the challenging stride of the family on women through her book, *A Woman in Her War Room, Breaking through Silence in Marriage*. The book highlights the family, the woman as a mother and wife, in her silent moments, the experiences in silent battles, and what family is in our society.

Being a mother and a wife along with her role as a Minister of the gospel and gender advocate, Apostle Dr. Pedro viewed this concept with a warm, loving heart and took the step to bring this book as a solution resource to women's roles as wives and mothers in facing challenges around them.

Marriage and Family have challenged many women in their calling to advance their inherent roles in the family, ministry, and society. As a result, women's roles and responsibilities express imperfections and flaws. Therefore, they soak themselves in silence and lack the skills or weapons to break it. The time is now for us to escape from the victim mode to journey on the victory road as women, wives, and mothers.

Through the pages, this book provides the empowerment-strength and knowledge to break the barriers of silence emanating from a woman's war room. Reading through the pages with an open mind and pure heart will enable you to overcome the obstacles through your war room and rise to break through the silence.

Apostle Dr. Pedro, I am strengthened by the inspiration of this book, and I appreciate you the more. I am convinced that this book will be a great resource to women worldwide and wish that it will continue to sing the mantra of leading women in marriage, family, community, and Ministry accordingly to allow their wounded hearts to become the tablet for another woman. The time has come for a Woman in Her War Room: Breaking through the Silence to adequately overcome accrued imperfection and flaws and advance her inherent potential. Keep on the Good Work, Apostle Dr. Elizabeth Pedro.

Professor Ada JUNI Okika,
Ph.D, FOIE, D-SPC, CDKA
Rector, Ruth Sisters' Fellowship International.

INTRODUCTION

"A strong woman is the lifeline of her family. She carries within her the power to endure pain and the courage to sacrifice."

WE ARE WARRIORS

I am happy with the success of the first edition of this series - **"A WOMAN IN HER WAR ROOM (How to Be a Powerful Woman)."** The first edition extensively explained the coming of the woman, how the world received her, and the wars she is currently fighting. I urge you to order the book today if you don't have it yet. In the first edition, are expositions you never knew about the woman. It is a compelling masterpiece that can transform your thinking about who you are. I must say it is a sure bet because testimonies are coming from different parts of the world already, attesting to the transformational power of the first edition. Get it now to understand this second edition significantly better.

In this second edition, I will discuss how to break through silence in marriage as a woman. Believe me when I say there are silent moments (a situation that you feel is shameful and embarrassing to discuss or share outside your marriage) in almost more than 80%

of homes in our society today. As women, we have buttoned up a lot, which has kept us mute, affecting how we relate in society. Do you doubt it? Read on to the last page of this book to see for yourself.

This book shall reveal the origin of the family and the concept of marriage. Many of us make mistakes in marriage because we lack the original knowledge of what a marriage is in the first place. Some people get married because they saw others do so while growing up. Others are in it because they want to bear children and make their parents grannies. Many are in it because they made a mistake that resulted in marrying to keep their integrity intact. There are so many reasons why people get married. Hearing most of these reasons brings tears to my eyes because I am particularly concerned about building better and stronger families.

Marriage is a beautiful thing. Marriage is the intimate union and equal partnership of a man and a woman. It comes to us from the hand of God, who created male and female in His image so that they might become one body and might be fertile and multiply (See Genesis chapters 1 and 2). Though man and woman are equal as God's children, they are created with significant differences that allow them to give themselves and to receive the other as a gift.

Marriage is both a natural institution and a sacred union because it is rooted in the divine plan of creation. In addition, the Catholic Church teaches that the valid marriage between two baptized Christians is a sacrament – a saving reality and a symbol of Christ's love for His church (See Ephesians 5:25-33). In every marriage, the spouses make a contract with each other. In a sacramental marriage, the couple also enters into a covenant in which their love is sealed and strengthened by God's love.

The free consent of the spouses makes a marriage. From this consent and the sexual consummation of marriage, a special bond arises between husband and wife. This bond is lifelong and exclusive. God has established the marriage bond and so it cannot be dissolved.

> **GOD HAS ESTABLISHED THE MARRIAGE BOND AND SO IT CANNOT BE DISSOLVED.**

At the same time, we know that marriage itself is not a magic wand. Getting married won't automatically make you a happy person. In fact, you can gain similar benefits from other kinds of relationships with friends and relatives. In building a happier life, women and men all have something better than magic. We have the ability to learn the specific skills we need to forge and maintain better relationships of all kinds.

This book focuses on marriage from the woman's point of view and her activities in it. It shall go deep into opening up silent moments of the woman in her marriage. Many women die in silence, while others are pushed to do unimaginable things. Sometimes depression sets in, and some extreme cases have led to suicides.

Many do not know this because they are blessed with a good spouse. Reading this book will help you to be grateful for your marriage as a woman, and for those going through silent moments, you shall find succour, take up your piece and fight to win.

CHAPTER ONE

THE ORIGIN OF THE FAMILY

"For this reason, a man will leave his father and mother and be united to his wife, and the two will become one flesh."
Ephesians 5:31 (NIV)

The word family is a single word with many different definitions depending on the context in which it is used. People have many ways of defining a family and what being a part of a family means to them. Families can be seen from different facets. It could be from the economic, cultural, social, and many other facets, but what every family has in common is that the people who call it their family are committed to being faithful to each other.

DEFINITION OF THE WORD FAMILY

The dictionary defines family in several ways. One definition says a family is "a fundamental social group in society typically consisting of one or two parents and their children." While this definition is a good starting point, several modern family structures are excluded by this definition, such as childless couples or other variations on the family unit. Another definition says, "Two or more people who share goals and values, have long-term commitments to one another, and usually reside in the same dwelling.

The family is the most universal and fundamental social institution that performs various societal functions.

The first family ever recorded was instituted by the first man and woman in this world, Adam and Eve. This is confirmed in the Bible, which says a man will leave his father and mother and shall now live with his wife.

Genesis 2:23-24 puts it this way:

> ²³*And the man said: "This is now bone of my bones and flesh of my flesh; she shall be called 'woman,' for out of man she was taken." ²⁴For this reason, a man will leave his father and his mother and be united to his wife, and they will become one flesh.*

FUNCTION OF A FAMILY

It is in the record that different sociologists have viewed or classified the functions of the family into different types. Below are the few I will want us to look at. It is important you know because it will be a good thing first to have actual knowledge of the function of a family.

MacIver has divided the functions of a family into **essential** and **non-essential** types. There are three main ESSENTIAL functions such as stable satisfaction of sex needs, production and rearing of children, and a provision of a home. But besides these MacIverian family functions, the family may also perform some other essential functions. But it must be remembered that essential functions are those functions which are fundamental, and no other institutions can perform these functions as successfully as the family can. However, the family performs the following essential functions:

1. STABLE SATISFACTION OF SEXUAL NEEDS

This is the most important essential function of the family. The family has been performing these functions since the inception of human civilization. It is well known that the sex urge is the human being most important and powerful instinct and natural urge. It is the primary duty of the family to satisfy the sexual appetite of its members in a stable and desirable way.

Through the mechanism of marriage, the family regulates the sexual behavior of its members because the satisfaction of sex instincts brings about the desire for a lifelong partnership between husband and wife. Satisfying sex needs in a marriage in a desirable way

> **SATISFYING SEX NEEDS IN A MARRIAGE IN A DESIRABLE WAY HELPS IN THE NORMAL DEVELOPMENT OF THE PERSONALITIES OF THOSE INVOLVED.**

helps in the normal development of the personalities of those involved.

Ancient Hindu Philosophers Manu and Vatsayan opine that the satisfaction of sex needs is the primary objective of the family. If it is suppressed, it creates personality maladjustments.

2. PROCREATION AND REARING OF CHILDREN

It is another vital section of the family. The family provides the legitimate basis for the production of children. It institutionalizes the process of procreation. By performing this function of procreation, the family contributes to its continuity and, ultimately, the human race.

Hence perpetuation of the human race or society is the most essential function of the family. The production of children and child-rearing is another vital family function. The family is the only place where the role of child-rearing is better performed.

It provides food, shelter, affection, protection, and security to all its members. It plays a vital role in the process of socialization of the child. It provides a healthy atmosphere in which the child's personality develops appropriately. The family takes care of the child's needs. Hence it is rightly remarked that the family is an institution par excellence for the procreation and rearing of children. It has no parallels.

3. PROVISION OF HOME

The family performs another important function of providing all its members a home for common living. It is only in a home that children are born and brought up.

Even if children are born in hospitals in these modern times, they are still cared for and adequately nourished in a home only because the family and a home have no substitutes. In a home, all the family members live together, and a child is brought up under the strict vigilance of all its members.

> **EVEN IF CHILDREN ARE BORN IN HOSPITALS IN THESE MODERN TIMES, THEY ARE STILL CARED FOR AND ADEQUATELY NOURISHED IN A HOME ONLY BECAUSE THE FAMILY AND A HOME HAVE NO SUBSTITUTES.**

All the members need a home to live happily in with comfort, peace, and protection. A home provides emotional and psychological support to all its members. Man's necessity for love and human response is fulfilled here.

The family provides recreation to its members. In a home, the family performs the role of a modern club. Man gets peace by living in a home.

4. SOCIALIZATION

It is another important essential function of the family. It is said that man is not born human but made human. Newborn human babies become human beings after they are socialized. Family plays an essential role in the socialization process. It is one of the primary agents of socialization. A baby learns norms, values, morals, and society's ideals by living in a family. He learns the culture and acquires character through the process of socialization. His personality develops in the course of his living in a family. From the family, he learns what is right and wrong and what is good or bad. Through socialization, he becomes a social man and acquires good character.

NON-ESSENTIAL OR SECONDARY FUNCTIONS OF FAMILY

As we have seen, famous Sociologist MacIver has divided functions into essential and non-essential parts. Under non-essential or secondary functions, he includes economic, religious, educational, health, and recreational functions.

Along with the essential functions, the family also performs these non-essential functions. These functions are non-essential or secondary in the sense that these are also performed simultaneously by other social institutions in the family. These functions are:

1. ECONOMIC FUNCTIONS

The family is an important economic unit. Since ancient times the family has been performing several economic functions; the family was both a production and consumption unit. It used to provide almost all the economic needs of its members, such as food, clothing, housing, etc. In those days, the family was self-sufficient. But nowadays, almost all the economic functions of the family are performed by other agencies, and the family only remains as a consumption unit. It does not produce anything. All the members of the family now work outside the home. But despite all these, the family still performs some economic functions of purchasing, protecting, and maintaining property. It also equally distributes property among its members.

2. EDUCATIONAL FUNCTIONS

Family performs many educational functions for its members. As a primary educational institution, the family is expected to teach all its members letters, knowledge, skill, and trade secrets. It looks after the primary education of its members and moulds their careers and character. The mother acts as the first and best teacher of a child. Besides, he learns all sorts of informal education from the family, such as discipline, obedience, manners, etc. But of course, it's worth mentioning that many of the educational functions of the family today have been taken over by schools, colleges, and universities. Still, the family continues to play an essential role in providing its members with the first lessons and primary education.

3. RELIGIOUS FUNCTIONS

The family is the centre of all religious activities. Family members can choose to offer their prayers together and observe different religious rites, rituals, and practices jointly. All the members may believe in a particular religion and decide to observe religious ceremonies at home. Children get to learn different religious values from their parents. Living in a healthy spiritual atmosphere helps develop spirituality among the children.

The family transmits religious beliefs and practices from one generation to another. But sadly, today, the family is becoming more and more secular, with religion having less and less influence in our daily lives.

Still, the family continues to play an important role in shaping the religious attitude of its members.

4. HEALTH-RELATED FUNCTIONS

As a primary social group, the family performs several health-related functions for its members. It looks after the health and vigor of its members. It takes care of the sick, the old, or aged persons of the family.

By providing necessary nutritive food to its members, the family takes care of the health of all. The family organizes different festivals, which are other sources of recreation. The relationship between grandparents and grandchildren is another source of entertainment. In the past, after the day's work, all the family members used to assemble and exchange their experiences and opinions. But today, clubs have replaced many recreational functions of the family. But at the same time, it is said that the present family acts as a modern club without evil effects.

5. CULTURAL FUNCTIONS

The family also performs several cultural functions as well. It preserves different cultural traits. Man learns and acquires culture from family and transmits it to succeeding generations. That is why the family is considered the centre of culture.

6. SOCIAL FUNCTIONS

The family performs many social functions. It teaches the coming generations social customs traditions, norms, and etiquette.

The family exercises social control over its members and brings them into conformity with accepted standards. Senior members of the family directly control the children's behavior, making them good citizens.

You must understand the above so that when we discuss the battles women fight in the subsequent chapters, you will understand why they are battles to be fought and won.

Having understood the reason for a family, let us discuss what "**Marriage**" is.

WHAT IS MARRIAGE?

Marriage is the intimate union and equal partnership of a man and a woman. It comes to us from the hand of God, who created male and female in His image so that they might become one body and be fertile and multiply (See Genesis chapters 1 and 2). Though man and woman are equal as God's children, they are created with significant differences that allow them to offer themselves and receive each other as gifts.

Marriage is both a natural institution and a sacred union because it is rooted in the divine plan of creation. In addition, the Catholic Church teaches that the valid marriage between two baptized Christians is a sacrament – a saving reality and a symbol of Christ's love for His church (See Ephesians 5:25-33).

In every marriage, the spouses make a contract with each other. In a sacramental marriage, the couple also enters into a covenant in which their love is sealed and strengthened by God's love.

The free consent of the spouses makes a marriage. From this consent and the sexual consummation of marriage, a special bond arises between husband and wife. This bond is lifelong and exclusive. God has established the marriage bond, so it cannot be dissolved.

The mutual love of a married couple should always be open to new life. This openness is expressed powerfully in the sexual union of husband and wife.

> **THE MUTUAL LOVE OF A MARRIED COUPLE SHOULD ALWAYS BE OPEN TO NEW LIFE. THIS OPENNESS IS EXPRESSED POWERFULLY IN THE SEXUAL UNION OF HUSBAND AND WIFE.**

The power to create a child with God is at the heart of what spouses share in sexual intercourse. Mutual love includes the mutual gift of fertility. Couples who cannot conceive or are beyond their child-bearing years can still express openness to life. They can share their generative love with grandchildren, other children and families, and the wider community.

As a result of their new nature in Christ, all Christians are called to a life of holiness. This divine calling, or vocation, can be lived in marriage, the single life, the priesthood, or consecrated (religious) life. No one vocation is superior to or inferior to another. Each involves a specific kind of commitment that flows from one's gifts and is further strengthened by God's grace. All vocations uniquely contribute to the Church's life and mission.

The family arises from marriage. Parents, children, and family members form a domestic church or church of the home. This is the primary unit of the Church – the place where the Church lives in the daily love, care, hospitality, sacrifice, forgiveness, prayer, and faith of ordinary families.

> **THE FAMILY IS THE PRIMARY UNIT OF THE CHURCH.**

GOD'S BLUEPRINT FOR A SUCCESSFUL MARRIAGE

God's step-by-step plan for a successful marriage is given in Ephesians 5:18–33. The first step in following God's design for married couples is to be filled with the Spirit. To attempt to do what God is telling you to do without the Holy Spirit's help is impossible. The calling of God is the enabling of God. Before a word is said about wives submitting to their husbands, both spouses are commanded to "submit to one another in the fear of God" (Eph. 5:21).

> **TO ATTEMPT TO DO WHAT GOD IS TELLING YOU TO DO WITHOUT THE HOLY SPIRIT'S HELP IS IMPOSSIBLE.**

The word for *submit* means "to get in order under something." In a military sense, it means to rank beneath and under. Wives must submit to their husband's loving leadership. Though Paul starts with the ladies first, in the roles and responsibilities of the marriage partners, it is clear that the wife's submissiveness can and will be a response to the husband's godly and loving leadership. A husband is not to treat his wife as a servant or a child but as an equal for whom God has given him the responsibility to care, provide for, love, and protect.

CHAPTER TWO

THE WOMAN IN HER MARRIAGE

Then the Lord God said, "It is not good that the man should be alone; I will make him a helper fit for him."
(Genesis 2:18)

Marriage is a beautiful thing. Behind every successful man is a woman. And if the man is married, then the woman is definitely his wife.

The role of a wife is so crucial that she can either make or break a family. She gives her husband the strength to succeed, she nurtures her children to stay healthy and do well in their life, and she has the ability to take care of every minute detail at home.

God designed marriage to be between two people physically born into this world, male and female. God intended for marriage to be a place of love and care, where sexual needs are satisfied and where both partners treat each other with respect and equality.

> **GOD DESIGNED MARRIAGE TO BE BETWEEN TWO PEOPLE PHYSICALLY BORN INTO THIS WORLD, MALE AND FEMALE.**

Marriage started with Adam and Eve in the Garden of Eden. Life and times of today have changed, empowering women and liberating them from centuries of oppression, financial inferiority, and relative anonymity in building social guidelines. More than ever in the history of mankind, our times have seen women rise as a force not just as a gender but as valid members of the human race who must have an equal voice, rights, and access to opportunities. This isn't to ignore several occasions when the glass ceilings still exist. But they're consistently being broken to positive applause.

With these, however, also comes a new-found sense of a woman's role in shaping the fortunes and direction of a family. It is no longer news that a good woman guarantees a good family resulting in a good society.

> **A GOOD WOMAN GUARANTEES A GOOD FAMILY RESULTING IN A GOOD SOCIETY.**

Not only does she complement her spouse and help him grow, but she also educates the children, tends to the older generation, and turns around the entire cultural edifice in which a family and a group of people might revolve.

The unique responsibilities of a wife make her role far more challenging than many corporate offices can offer. A woman is not only equipped to handle the toughest of them emotionally, but they are streets ahead physically too, a feat of endurance most men would struggle to match.

The loving, servant leadership role, as emphasized by a husband in traditional family structures, provides a perfect counterpoint and a good marker of how a good wife can make all the difference in a relationship, making it stronger.

THE ROLE OF THE WOMAN AS A WIFE

THE ROLE OF A WIFE

Marriage transforms a woman's life; from a pampered, carefree girl, she evolves into a responsible woman ready to take on the duties of a wife. Let's see what those duties are:

1. LOVE HIM UNCONDITIONALLY
In a marriage, a man wants to be liked, loved, and appreciated, just like a woman does. As a wife, give unconditional love to your husband physically and emotionally. Appreciate him generously and nurture him as your child. And what do you get in return? His unconditional love, of course.

2. HELP HIM
Who said men don't need help? All of us need help and support. Become your husband's helping hand during tough times. Whenever he seeks your help, be proactive in supporting him. He will do the same when you require his assistance.

3. KEEP HIS HONOR/DIGNITY

Don't talk negatively about your husband to your family, friends, or relatives. Don't fight with him or criticize him in front of others. Don't indulge in gossiping about your husband. If you have any issues, sort them out between you.

4. SUPPORT HIM

A wife should stand by her husband so they can work together as a team. Whether in daily routines or in achieving long-term goals, you need to support your husband in all his ventures and endeavors. He will be glad to have you beside him in every step.

5. BE AVAILABLE

A wife needs her husband's company, and a husband needs his wife's. Be there for him when he wants to talk to you. Listen to him and advise him if required, and take care of his needs. It shows that you love and care for him.

> **A WIFE NEEDS HER HUSBAND'S COMPANY, AND A HUSBAND NEEDS HIS WIFE'S.**

6. RESPECT HIM

Respect is mutual. Value his opinions and respect him for who he is. If you disagree with him, do not disrespect him but put across your point softly. When you give respect, you earn respect.

7. FULFIL HIS NEEDS

Seeing your husband depend on you like a child is amusing and sometimes annoying. Don't be surprised if your husband can't find the things right before him, and seek your help to find them.

Don't wonder why he doesn't appreciate your presence; instead, go away for two days and see how much he will miss you. A wife is that important to fulfil a man's needs.

8. BE FAITHFUL TO YOUR HUSBAND

Once married, you have to remain loyal and committed to your husband, no matter what. Do not give him a reason to question your faithfulness. And expect the same from him.

9. SEEK HIS OPINION

When you seek your husband's opinion, it doesn't make you inferior. In fact, it shows you value his opinion and respect him.

10. COOK FOR HIM

Dish out healthy meals for your husband as well as for you. Avoid the temptation of grabbing some junk food on the way to work. You may ask your husband to help you in the kitchen, which could be a good way to spend more time with each other.

11. RESPECT YOUR IN-LAWS

Irrespective of the differences in culture or lifestyle, respect your husband's parents, siblings, and relatives as you would want him to respect yours.

12. TAKE CARE OF HOUSEHOLD DUTIES

Keep the house in order, tidy and clean. Seek help from your husband and children. Assign them some duties to carry out every day. This way, each person feels responsible for their role in the family.

13. BE RESPONSIBLE

A responsible wife is a blessing to the family because she knows what to do and how to do it. Be responsible in running the household, managing your finances, and taking care of your children.

14. BE PATIENT

Patience doesn't come easily. When you multitask every day at home, and things don't go as you plan, the last thing you think about is patience. But try having it, and you will not regret it.

Imagine you are hurrying to work, your husband asks you something silly, and you shush him. But later in the day, you realize he only tried to be playful with you. Had you been more patient in the morning, the day would have been better for you and your husband.

15. SAFEGUARD YOUR HOME

You must protect your home from strangers and people who try to inject venomous thoughts into your family members. Also, keep away from individuals with a lot of negativity.

16. TAKE CARE OF YOURSELF

No, this is not the last thing to do. In fact, you should focus on yourself before you take care of others because your family can be happy and healthy only if you are happy and healthy. Don't burden yourself with responsibilities. Seek help from the others in the family, take a break, and relax. This will keep you smiling; a smiling wife is the most pleasing thing for a husband to see.

THE ROLE OF THE WOMAN AS A MOTHER IN THE FAMILY

MY ROLE AS A MOTHER

A solid marriage can support and nurture all members of the family. Acting as a mother in the family is totally different from acting as a wife to a husband. Being a

> **ACTING AS A MOTHER IN THE FAMILY IS TOTALLY DIFFERENT FROM ACTING AS A WIFE TO A HUSBAND.**

mother is a whole other job altogether. Many of you mothers can bear me witness that it is a whole different role to play in being a mother and another in being a wife.

As a wife, you basically deal with just your husband and slightly his family members. Dealing with individuals who see things differently and trying to love them without feeling less important is a whole job. Thus as a woman, this is the most difficult for me. Putting up all effort to be seen as a good mother by my children is my focus each morning.

This is not all there is to the woman's role as a mother in the family, but I will do justice by listing a few.

1. PROTECTING THE GIRLS RATHER THAN OVERPROTECTING THEM
As mothers, we must find a balance to have a healthy family. Do not overprotect a particular gender of children over another. Most times, this causes problems in the family. When girls are overprotected, sons may feel unloved.

2. GIVING ATTENTION TO EACH CHILD BEFORE THEY NEEDED IT
Share special times doing things they enjoy—quality and quantity time and providing spiritual training,

cultural opportunities, and creative outlets appropriate for their ages, abilities, and interests.

3. VALUING EACH CHILD AS AN INDIVIDUAL BECAUSE GOD MADE EACH ONE SO WONDERFULLY DIFFERENT!
Each child is unique, with unique features. God made them different, and they react to things differently. It is the role of the mother to understand this and treat them according to who they are and not in any way despise them for who they are.

4. BEING PROUD WHEN THEY PUT FORTH EFFORT — WHETHER OR NOT THEY EXCEL.
Don't only concentrate on the outcome of their actions; focus more on their effort to get what you see as an outcome. The truth is the desired result can be achieved when a reasonable attempt is administered. The mother has to know how to bring out the best in any child of hers.

5. NOT COMPARING!
This is what destroys families and sets the children up against each other. A mother should be cautious not to ignite a fire she won't be there to put out. I have seen families divide because the mum compares the activities of child A with those of child B or even an

> **THE DAY A MOTHER ALLOWS THE COMPARING SPIRIT INTO HER FAMILY, SHE SIGNS A CONTRACT TO SELF-DESTROY HER FAMILY.**

external child who is not a family member. The day a mother allows this comparing spirit into her family, she signs a contract to self-destroy her family.

6. HELPING OUR CHILDREN UNDERSTAND THAT DIFFERENT SEASONS OF LIFE HAVE DIFFERENT NEEDS.

Not all children understand that different seasons in life have different needs. It is the place of parents, especially mothers, to make their children understand this, especially those not yet grown up.

7. TEACH THEM THAT LIFE ISN'T ALWAYS FAIR...

Teach them that while life isn't always fair, God gives us what we really need and the ability to handle it. Psalm 138:8: "God will accomplish what concerns me."

8. RESPECTING OUR DAUGHTERS' INDIVIDUAL SOCIAL LIVES WHILE TRAINING THEM TO CARE FOR OUR SONS.

Those with older daughters who are big enough to take care of other siblings should never expect the care they give the younger ones to be "their job." We must consider arranging payments for such a caretaking job. We must allow our daughters to experience freedom and responsibility but never feel we are taking advantage of their "free" services. As we respect their young lives, they become helpful, compassionate women who love their younger siblings and want to care for them.

Marriage becomes a beautiful journey when you provide for, nurture, and complement each other. As a wife, you might want to give it your best shot while maintaining your dignity and self-respect.

CHAPTER THREE

SILENT MOMENTS OF THE WOMAN IN HER MARRIAGE

Hannah was so sad that she cried the whole time she was praying to the LORD. She made a special promise to God and said, "LORD All-Powerful, you can see how sad I am. **(1 Samuel 1:10-11)**

Marriage was designed by God in creation to meet certain fundamental needs of the human being, which we have done justice to in chapters one and two of this book. When those needs are richly met, every marriage flourishes.

The Marriage Covenant is the structural principle of holding weak and fickle human beings to the promises they have made. When the marriage covenant is strongly built, it provides a stable and enduring context for pursuing the Creators' blessings of companionship, sex, and family partnership. It can reach the pinnacle of what God created humans to be.

Sadly the story does not always go this way. In fact, it seems as though it does not often go this way. I have seen marriages become a place of misery instead of joy. A husband or wife wakes up each morning with a heavy heart, saddened by the perception that the marriage is not working, perhaps even terrified by the oppression they experience. It is called "Silent Moments in our marriages."

Nobody tells the engaged or newly married couple to expect that marriage will not always be blissful. They are loaded with a lot of ways to make homes blissful.

This leaves couples poorly prepared for the suffering that inevitably comes in marriages, and when these silent moments hit them, the couple is bewildered. Many who cannot handle the heat of these moments are tempted to abandon the marriage and seek relief for their pain. They also forget that abandoning a marriage on its own creates new suffering.

Marital suffering can lead to extreme spiritual anguish, physical distress, and social isolation. This suffering is subjective and full of personal experience. Different couples endure different pain even though they are enduring the same marriage. Harsh words may hurt one spouse more than the other. Chronic lack of communication, lack of sexual intimacy, or lack of spiritual partnership could be experienced as deeply painful by one spouse and not by the other. An act of sexual infidelity or violence may be experienced as creating unbearable suffering, or it may not, depending on the way individual spouses interpret and react to these particular painful events.

The experience of marital suffering can often be linked to marital expectations or desires. Short of objective physical or emotional violence, we suffer in marriage when the experience we are having falls short of our expectations.

Suffering can enter marriage through several channels. Due to my relationship with women, I have heard and seen a lot of ugly experiences women go through. I will be dealing extensively on the battles our young ladies fight in their marriages due to pressures to get married by their families, peer pressures, etc.

EARLY MARRIAGE BATTLE

Many ladies have been forced into early marriages without being prepared for it. Marriage, in the eyes of many, is seen to be a coming together of two people (man and woman) who agree to live together as husband and wife, give birth to as many children as possible, with the man having the responsibility of taking care of the wife's entire family.

The rate at which child marriages are allowed in some parts of the world is heartbreaking. Young girls are allowed to go through a lot of pain simply because, from nowhere, one man is interested in marrying them. Imagine the girl who is not mature enough to even take care of herself completely now being forced to care not only for herself but for a man expecting her to be perfect overnight. My heart melts when I hear what these young ones go through in marriage at their tender age. Tell me, what will be their story about life if asked? They weren't allowed to live like other privileged girls out there. They are not allowed to live and express themselves, dream, make mistakes, learn from them, and choose who or not to marry. Their lives are truncated, and a totally different life is handed over to them to live.

I would love us in some seconds to imagine what this young child will be going through in her marriage. Because of her immaturity, there are tendencies of violations, abuse, complications in childbirth, and any other thing you could possibly imagine in your head right now.

Gender equality is a fundamental human right and an important pillar for a peaceful, prosperous, and sustainable world. The boy and girl child are human and need to be treated the same.

Child marriage, to me, violates the rights of children in a way that often leads to a lifetime of disadvantages. It is immeasurable. It brings with it also a lot of deprivation in the life of our girls. The child may experience assaults, physical and mental health challenges and have little or no decision-making power within the household, especially when married to an older man.

> **CHILD MARRIAGE VIOLATES THE RIGHTS OF CHILDREN IN A WAY THAT OFTEN LEADS TO A LIFETIME OF DISADVANTAGES.**

MARRIAGE FOR MONEY

In many parts of Africa, young ladies are forced to marry. This singular reason has led to many sad outcomes in marriages across Africa. As naive as they are, they are entangled with a man who will treat them the way they desire and go free because they care for the woman's family. Her family won't even have the audacity to confront the man on the maltreatment of their daughter because, to them, he is a saviour. They would rather advise their daughter to endure the pain she is perpetually placed in to keep her family members happy. What a way to kill the woman's pride because nobody could fight for her.

I heard the story of a young lady whose family gave her out in marriage to a man against her will simply because the man promised to help train the male children of her family. Women in this situation are often bitter and, most times, wish their husbands would die so they can be set free.

BARRENNESS IN MARRIAGES

This is another battle that a woman fights in her marriage. It is common now in our societies, but the pain that comes with the stigma is severe. While preparing for this subtopic, I stumbled upon a story online and wish to share it with you.

When Cecilia Wairimu was growing up, she hoped she would marry and bring up her own family upon reaching adulthood. At least, that is what her upbringing taught her. And so when she cleared school and was old enough, she met and married a man in the church in a colourful wedding ceremony.

"All was well between us until a year later when there was nothing to show for the union. We had wished for a baby, but there was none," she recalls. When the second year came, and there was still no child, their love became a domestic tinderbox. "It worried me that I could not have a child: first, because I really wanted to be a mother, and second because it was a shameful thing not being able to carry a pregnancy," Wairimu says. The couple disagreed on many other things, but childlessness seemed to be the leading cause of all their troubles.

The blame was automatically laid on her. Even her mother-in-law called her barren. She took it in her stride, visiting a gynaecologist afterwards for diagnosis and possible treatment. "I asked my husband to come with me to the hospital. He was reluctant but finally agreed. I was diagnosed with blocked tubes, and him with low sperm count. He was given medicine to take continuously, but he stopped six months later," she says.

By year five and without a child, the couple had grown apart. Wairimu's husband abused her physically and verbally. No form of counselling helped. When Wairimu couldn't take it anymore, she quit the marriage. While the pain of an abusive marriage ceased, that of childlessness never stopped.

Such is the agony of not being able to bear a child in a society where the yardstick for manliness and womanliness is the ability to conceive and bring forth new life.

Cecilia Wairimu ended up in a second marriage, which lasted three years. This marriage also ended because of the same problem of being unable to bear a child. She had visited a gynaecologist a second time and was further diagnosed with fibroids and was operated on again.

"After the second marriage, I was feeling exhausted. I was numb. Not being able to get a child had hurt so much that I no longer felt anything. After the two marriages, I had effectively given up on the prospects of motherhood," she says.

She continued living her life – rebuilding where the endless pursuit of a baby held her back. But then a suitor came calling – a man with genuine interest: "I decided to give him a chance, but not because I was still hoping for a baby: I was happy to have a companion."

At some point, after being with the man for some time, Wairimu missed her periods. She didn't think much about it but later decided to test for pregnancy which turned out positive.

I also wish to share other painful moments women go through in their marriages. In addition, I will tell the story of my younger sister, to whom I am dedicating this book.

Veronica's STORY

A 22-year-old woman, Veronica Boniface, in Nassarawa State, was arrested by the Nigeria Security and Civil Defence Corps (NSCDC) for stabbing her husband to death following a purported phone conversation with a 'strange woman.'

Mohammed Mahmoud-Fari, the state commandant of the NSCDC, said the suspect was arrested on Tuesday after allegedly committing the act. According to him, the suspect stabbed her late husband with a kitchen knife following an argument about a phone call from a purported strange woman.

The suspect, a mother of one currently pregnant, revealed her intention was to scare her late husband and collect the phone but mistakenly ended up killing him. According to her, she was using the knife to peel yam before the altercation and mistakenly stabbed her husband in a bid to collect the phone from him." She regretted her action and pleaded for forgiveness.

The above story is very touching because, from the details, one can tell this was a young marriage. And I am tempted to ask, where is the love that started the relationship?

For her to have reacted in such a manner meant the situation had probably gotten out of hand for her to bear anymore. Maybe she had confronted him before, but he denied it, and instead of seeking help, she decided to act irrationally this time, killing her husband as a result.

STORY 2

A man beats his wife up because she questioned him over a phone conversation with another woman. He beat her up, posted it on his Facebook page, and said he was waiting for the police. He was eventually arrested, and it was discovered that the lady in question was pregnant for him.

Imagine such wickedness: beating up your pregnant wife and posting it on social media. Now the man's family members are blaming the woman, asking why she didn't delete the post her husband made upon seeing it.

What a family! No wonder their son thinks he can act anyhow and go free. Why will a man in his right senses raise his hand on his pregnant wife and post the video on social media? This shows what a sick individual he is, and instead of his family begging and thinking of how to take him to a mental hospital for help, they've chosen the blame game.

Women go through this in many other places and are silent about it.

STORY 3

Tragedy mostly hovers around us humans as vultures would do over a dying animal. More often than not, it catches us pants down. We need to be careful all the time. The thought of death was not one of Eddie's thoughts on the night he died. He had gone out on that fateful day as he will always do. He returned home at past 8 p.m.

His wife ignored all entreaties by him to open the door. She was quoted as asking the husband to return to wherever he came from. She had repeatedly complained about her husband's late homecoming.

The man was determined to sleep in his room. He attempted to open the door through the window. Unfortunately, he suffered a cut. One of the veins was affected. He shouted, please open the door for me; I have sustained an injury. The woman was adamant. He gave up the effort and went back to his car to sleep.

Little did he know it was a deadly wound he had suffered. He bled profusely. He was said to have been found dead in his car the following morning. I am sure his wife lives daily wishing she had opened the door for him that night.

I have always insisted that marriage should be built upon mutual respect. Why would a partner want to lock the door against the other partner in a home that only acquired the status of a home only because of the presence of the two parties living harmoniously together? It is not a home if no love flows from mutual trust and respect for each other. How does the locking of the door serve as a solution to any problem?

> **IT IS NOT A HOME IF NO LOVE FLOWS FROM MUTUAL TRUST AND RESPECT FOR EACH OTHER.**

It is strange that, in this particular case, the man was locked out. In the majority of cases, it is the woman who suffers the humiliation of being locked out. She is the one who is told to go back to where she is coming from. She is the one who never has a valid excuse for returning late to the house. Why must the vehicle she entered break down on the way? She should have told the car that her no-nonsense husband would not take any excuse for lateness to return home. She cannot stay too long in the market during the day because she is in trouble when her husband gets home before her. She is a 'nobody' in the house. Like domestic helpers, she must not be out when it is time to lock the door; otherwise, she would be asked to return to where she is coming from. While it hurts me that Eddie lost his life because of His wife's childish behavior, I can hear whisperings: how could she do such a thing? Didn't she know that the man owned the house? She is a witch. And all kinds of stuff like that.

I will not justify her actions of that night, far from it. It is condemnable. What she did was terrible, not because she is a woman. The act remains bad regardless of the gender of the deed. I have had to counsel women in their dozens who suffer such humiliation daily from their husbands.

One Sunday, a lady called me to complain that her husband had locked her outside, asking the children not to open the gate for her. While he was sleeping, she rushed to the market to buy some rice she intended to cook that day. The man had called her several times while she was in the market and threatened to deal with her when she returned. When she got home, she met the gate locked. She called her husband to let the children open the gate for her. But he responded by saying she should go back to where she was coming from because he didn't know where she was coming from.

She stood outside for only God knows how long. It took the intervention of her son before the husband agreed to open the gate. He said the condition for peace was for her to throw the rice in the trash can. She agreed to do so on the condition that he would refund her the money used. But this same husband would always go out and return between 1 a.m. and 3 a.m. dead drunk despite Covid19 and all the restrictions of movement that came with it.

Such men would not tolerate being asked by their wives where they are. You would hear them thundering: "Am I staying with you? Am I your houseboy? Maybe you want to return to your parents' house." Why do men treat women the way they would not like to be treated?

Every human being deserves to be treated with respect and dignity. Couples should stop this arrogance towards one another.

Eddie's wife has learned her lesson the sad way. Let us learn from this and stop treating our partners with contempt.

EVERY HUMAN BEING DESERVES TO BE TREATED WITH RESPECT AND DIGNITY.

Men should stop humiliating their wives before the children and the neighbors. Each time women come home late, the usual story is that they have gone to see their ex-boyfriends. But the men can act as they will. Does God have different ethical codes for men and women? We all must be responsible in our conduct. Let no man decide to be an unauthorized enforcer of the code of conduct that only women should observe.

The next story I will share I am directly related to. It's about my sister. I didn't know what she was going through until when she died. It was an excruciating moment for me.

My kid sister was married and had no child four years into her marriage. Because of this, she started having issues with her mother-in-law. Pressure came from all in-laws. Five years later, the same story continued. She went through hell at the hands of her in-laws. She later got pregnant and had her first child. She had a second, a third, and a fourth child. My sister was going through a lot at the hands of her husband, and she never told me.

Her husband yelled at her for every slight mistake, and she said nothing or shared her misery with anyone.

My sister loved me so much that she would share anything with me except what she was going through in her marriage. I include her story in my book to help other women not to keep quiet or silent when they go through difficulties in their marriages.

My sister's husband would seize all the money I sent to her. Her husband did not let her go into the business we set up for her. She gave us different excuses. All these happened until a day I will never forget. That day she slumped and passed on. I was called 8-10 hours later. I told them to go to the hospital. She was already in a coma when they got there. One thing that shocked me was that the pastor referred to my sister as a transformer. He said, "Your sister was like a transformer."

You know how a transformer will absorb and absorb and then shuts down. I was so shocked when the pastor referred to her this way. That means the pastor knew what my sister was going through in her marriage but never did anything about it.

I am writing this to the clergy: no matter our titles, when someone comes to us with life-threatening marital issues, we should help them. Separation for a while can help both parties rather than let one die. That was how I lost my sister. She died, leaving behind four children. The last child was just twelve months when she passed on. That is why I am dedicating this book to my sister, Gladys.

CHAPTER FOUR

HOW TO FIGHT SILENT BATTLES IN YOUR HOME

Even the best marriages are occasionally bogged down by annoying but common grievances. These moments are very bad in marriages. For a woman in her marriage, moments like this could be caused by her husband, her children, her in-laws, or even herself, but the Good news is, you can fix them.

SILENT BATTLES CAUSED BY THE HUSBANDS

Women have gone through a lot at the hands of those they have married. They usually fight these silent battles alone because they fear being laughed at by their friends. They carry these burdens and, like the stories shared in chapter three of this book, get fed up, overwhelmed, and depressed. This may result in the women taking laws into their hands or remain victims of such moments. Below are some highlighted moments in marriages that make every woman mourn in her marriage. They might seem common and trivialized, but they can potentially destroy a family.

HE NEVER HELPS AROUND THE HOUSE

As a wife, you will bear me witness that there are moments when you feel your husband's help is needed in certain areas, and rather than helping out, he is telling you to your face that what you do is your sole responsibility. He would prefer to sit down than to help.

HE HARDLY KNOWS ANYTHING ABOUT THE KIDS

While studies have found that men interact with their children for at least three hours a day, many wives gripe that their guys don't know the day-to-day details of what's going on in their kids' lives. That's partially how they're wired: men communicate to exchange information, while women use it to bond, says Orlando.

Because of that, favorite movies, toys, or friends' names can sometimes be subconsciously dismissed as irrelevant information. Let your child handle the little lapses as long as your husband is on top of the big stuff.

WE HAVE THE SAME ARGUMENTS EVERY DAMN DAY

Every couple has a few arguments that seem to come up repeatedly. And that may not be a bad thing. A study found that "angry but honest" conversations can help marriages by stopping complaints from festering.

But if you find that you truly are hashing out the same issue all the time, it's worth sitting down and getting to the root of the problem.

HE DRINKS TOO MUCH

No woman wants a drunk for a husband. This alone is a huge battle fought by women in their families today caused by their husbands. Because of this, many women have been abused, disfigured, and subjected to humiliation. They tend to fight this in their closet because no woman can carry the stigma that comes with it when it is known to the public.

IT FEELS LIKE I CAN'T DO ANYTHING RIGHT

Experts say a single ratio separates great relationships from toxic ones: 5 to 1. That means that for every negative interaction you have, you should have five positive interactions. So if your husband constantly points out that the house is a mess, the kids are watching TV too much, or you aren't home enough, call his attention to his negativity to help him snap out of it.

HE'S AFRAID OF MY FEELINGS

Unfortunately, how men and women are wired often means partners have very different ways of expressing emotion. If you're upset, he may see your feelings as another problem for him to "fix." This can be incredibly frustrating for a wife just looking for a sympathetic ear and a shoulder to cry on.

HOW TO WIN THE HUSBAND-CAUSED BATTLE

There are tragedies of divorce—bitter ex-spouses, broken promises, and confused children. Don't let this happen to your family! Whether your marriage is going through tough times or is experiencing marital bliss—or even if you're not yet married but are considering it—the Bible offers proven guidance to help your marriage last. It's advice from God, the one who created and ordained marriage! If you've tried everything else, why not give Him a chance? Follow these Bible-proven instructions to get your marriage working.

HAVE YOUR OWN PRIVATE HOME

God's principle is that a married couple should move out of their parent's homes and establish their own, even if finances require something modest, such as a one-room apartment. A husband and wife should decide this together and remain firm even if someone opposes. Many marriages would be improved if this principle were carefully followed. Many wives have gone through tough times from their husbands' relations because they all live in the same house.

CONTINUE YOUR COURTSHIP

"Above all things have fervent love for one another, for 'love will cover a multitude of sins'" (1 Peter 4:8).

"Her husband … praises her" (Proverbs 31:28).

"She who is married cares … how she may please her husband" (1 Corinthians 7:34).

"Be kindly affectionate to one another … in honor giving preference to one another" (Romans 12:10).

Continue—or revive—your courtship into your marital life. Successful marriages don't just happen; they must be developed. Don't take one another for granted; the resulting monotony could harm your marriage. Keep your love for one another growing by expressing it to each other; otherwise, love might fade, and you could drift apart.

> **SUCCESSFUL MARRIAGES DON'T JUST HAPPEN; THEY MUST BE DEVELOPED.**

Love and happiness are not found by seeking them for yourself but by giving them to others. So spend as much time as possible doing things together. Learn to greet each other with enthusiasm.

Relax, visit, sightsee, and eat together. Don't overlook the little courtesies, encouragements, and affectionate acts. Surprise each other with gifts or favors. Try to "out-love" each other. **Don't try to take more out of your marriage than you put into it.** Lack of love is the biggest destroyer of marriage.

REMEMBER THAT GOD JOINED YOU TOGETHER IN MARRIAGE
"For this reason, a man shall leave his father and mother and be joined to his wife… So then, they are no longer two but one flesh. Therefore, what God has joined together, let not man

separate" (Matt. 19:5, 6). Has love nearly disappeared from your home? While the devil wants to break apart your marriage by tempting you to give up, don't forget that God joined you in marriage and desires you to stay together and be happy. He will bring happiness and love into your lives if you obey His divine commandments. *"With God, all things are possible"* (Matt. 19:26). Don't despair. God's Spirit can change your heart and your spouse's if you ask and let Him.

GUARD YOUR THOUGHTS

"As he thinks in his heart, so is he" (Proverbs 23:7).
"You shall not covet your neighbor's wife" (Exodus 20:17).

"Keep your heart with all diligence, for out of it spring the issues of life" (Proverbs 4:23).

"Whatever things are true ... noble ... just ... pure ... lovely ... of good report ... meditate on these things" (Philippians 4:8).

The wrong kind of thinking can profoundly harm your marriage. The devil will tempt you with thoughts like,

- "Our marriage was a mistake,"
- "She doesn't understand me,"
- "I can't take much more of this,"

- "We can always divorce if necessary,"
- "I'll go home to mother," or,
- "He smiled at that woman."

This kind of thinking is dangerous because your thoughts ultimately govern your actions. Avoid seeing, saying, reading, or hearing anything that—or associating with anyone who—suggests unfaithfulness on the part of your spouse. Thoughts uncontrolled are like an automobile left in neutral on a steep hill; the result could be disastrous.

> **THOUGHTS UNCONTROLLED ARE LIKE AN AUTOMOBILE LEFT IN NEUTRAL ON A STEEP HILL; THE RESULT COULD BE DISASTROUS.**

NEVER GO TO BED ANGRY WITH ONE ANOTHER
"Do not let the sun go down on your wrath" (Ephesians 4:26).

"Confess your trespasses to one another" (James 5:16).

"Forgetting those things which are behind" (Philippians 3:13).

"Be kind to one another, tenderhearted, forgiving one another, even as God in Christ forgave you" (Ephesians 4:32).

To remain angry over hurts and grievances—big or little—can be dangerous. Unless addressed promptly, even little problems can become set in your mind as convictions and can adversely affect your outlook on life. This is why God said to let your anger cool before going to bed. Be big enough to forgive and to say, "I'm sorry." After all, no one is perfect, and you are both on the same team, so be gracious enough to admit a mistake when you make it. Besides, making up is a very pleasant experience, with unusual powers to draw marriage partners closer together. God suggests it! It works!

> **BE BIG ENOUGH TO FORGIVE AND SAY, "I'M SORRY." ... BE GRACIOUS ENOUGH TO ADMIT A MISTAKE WHEN YOU MAKE IT.**

KEEP CHRIST IN THE CENTER OF YOUR HOME

"Unless the Lord builds the house, they labor in vain who build it" (Psalm 127:1).

"In all your ways acknowledge Him, and He shall direct your paths" (Proverbs 3:6).

"And the peace of God, which surpasses all understanding, will guard your hearts and minds through Christ Jesus" (Philippians 4:7).

This really is the greatest principle because it's the one that enables all the others. The vital ingredient of happiness in the home is not diplomacy, strategy, or our effort to overcome problems but rather a union with Christ. Hearts filled with Christ's love will not be far apart for long. With Christ in the home, marriage has a greater chance of success. Jesus can wash away bitterness and disappointment and restore love and happiness.

> **THE VITAL INGREDIENT OF HAPPINESS IN THE HOME IS NOT DIPLOMACY, STRATEGY, OR OUR EFFORT TO OVERCOME PROBLEMS BUT RATHER A UNION WITH CHRIST. HEARTS FILLED WITH CHRIST'S LOVE WILL NOT BE FAR APART FOR LONG.**

PRAY TOGETHER

"Watch and pray, lest you enter into temptation. The spirit indeed is willing, but the flesh is weak" (Matthew 26:41).

"Pray for one another" (James 5:16).

"If any of you lacks wisdom, let him ask of God, who gives to all liberally" (James 1:5).

Pray with/for one another! This wonderful activity will help your marriage succeed beyond your wildest dreams. Kneel before God and ask Him for true love for one another, forgiveness, strength, wisdom, and solutions to problems. God will answer. You won't be automatically cured of every fault, but God will have greater access to change your heart and actions.

HOW TO WIN IN-LAWS CAUSED BATTLES

A woman is expected to show her husband's parents and relations the respect and kindness that are due them from a dutiful daughter, while her husband must treat her parents with kindness at all times and under all circumstances. If we say that a woman is supposed to act in unison with her husband, then the least she may do is treat his parents with respect. Having said that, I should add that what we are talking about here is a genuine attitude manifested in behavior. Behavior, however, is different from service.

A woman is not required to serve her husband's parents. He is required to look after his parents and try as hard as possible to ensure their comfort according to his means. This means that if a woman decides to serve her husband's parents, in deference to them or out of love for her husband, she does so voluntarily. Her attitude should be met with gratitude by her husband and his parents, and her kindness should be reciprocated. But she violates no law or principle if she decides not to serve them. Her husband may not force or pressure her into serving them, whether they share the same house or live separately.

When we understand these limitations, the relationship between parents and their daughter-in-law acquires a different outlook. When someone does you a favor voluntarily, and you do not show your appreciation, they are bound to feel hurt. This is the experience of most women fighting these battles in their homes. There is no fight as draining as fighting ill-treatments and rejection from in-laws.

> **THERE IS NO FIGHT AS DRAINING AS FIGHTING ILL-TREATMENTS AND REJECTION FROM IN-LAWS.**

When a wife's kindness is returned or at least appreciated, she is encouraged to continue this generous attitude. But if, on the other hand, she is made to feel that a voluntary favor is expected of her as a duty when no religious or moral authority imposes it, then an attitude of rebellion begins to make itself felt.

Suppose a woman has young children and has to look after them. Nowadays, young children are too demanding, and the burden they present is quite a heavy one. Our modern times are different. In the past, a couple lived with their extended family, and a woman received the help she needed to raise her young children from the other women in the family.

If a woman has to serve her parents-in-law, she may find that she is required to work long hours without getting enough rest. There is also the possibility of conflict between your wife and parents. This may come about from the feeling that her service is not appreciated. As time goes on, this leads to strained relations and, probably, an outburst of anger from either side.

It isn't easy to remedy the situation when it reaches this stage. In such circumstances, a woman is within her right to ask her husband to move out of the family house. She wants to look after her immediate family and avoid frequent conflicts with her husband's parents. The advantage she sees in living alone is significant since she will be under no pressure and can organize her family to her satisfaction.

It is customary in certain societies that when the relationship within the family reaches this stage, the husband's parents may ask or suggest that he divorces his wife. Many divorce cases have sprung up because of disapproval from the woman's in-laws.

What should a husband do in such a case? If he acts on his parent's wishes, he will do his wife and himself a great wrong. He must not forget that he is duty-bound to look after his wife and give her a comfortable life according to his means. Therefore, he is responsible for looking after his wife and parents. If he cannot fulfill both obligations when he and his wife share the same house with his parents, it may be highly advisable for him to move out. And if this prompts his parents to ask him to divorce her, he must not do so, provided his wife fulfills her duties toward him, their children, and his parents. Once again, she is only obliged to treat them respectfully and kindly. Maybe when they move out, she would be better able to fulfill that duty and make it felt by them. This is a typical Oriental family problem. Islam has provided an easy solution, requiring everyone in the family to understand their duties and rights.

Some readers may feel that I am taking the wife's side. I wish to make it clear that I am not. I realize that some women are selfish and create problems within the family. A woman of this type should not be treated in the same way as a kind, dutiful woman who knows her rights and duties.

Based on this, a woman is within her right to ask her husband to provide her and their family with a separate home. She is also within her right if she decides not to serve her parents-in-law. It is wrong for parents to ask their son to divorce his wife because she does not serve them. Islam does not condone this provided she observes the duties enjoined upon her. Her husband must not act on his parents' wishes to divorce her because this would be a grave wrong.

> **IT IS WRONG FOR PARENTS TO ASK THEIR SON TO DIVORCE HIS WIFE BECAUSE SHE DOES NOT SERVE THEM.**

HOW TO WIN THE CHILDREN-CAUSED BATTLES

It is only natural for moms to wonder if they are doing an excellent job as moms. Constantly we ask ourselves questions like "**How can I be a good mom?**" and "**Am I a good mom?**" Many mothers always struggle with whether they are good moms to their kids. Taking care of children is a difficult task. Many women cry in their secret places daily and at night because of their children's behavior.

It's only natural to worry about our children. And whenever one of them does something wrong, we ask ourselves if we did anything to cause the behavior. In those times, we may wonder, "Am I a good mom?

WHO IS A GOOD MOTHER?

Many of us wonder, who is a good mother, and what qualities does she have? First of all, when we talk about who a good mother is, we need to realize this does not mean perfection! No mom is perfect, nor do we really want to be perfect, do we?

A good mother strives to be the best she can be. Along her journey of motherhood, she makes mistakes, admits them, then dusts herself off and tries again.

> **A GOOD MOTHER STRIVES TO BE THE BEST SHE CAN BE. ALONG HER JOURNEY OF MOTHERHOOD, SHE MAKES MISTAKES, ADMITS THEM, THEN DUSTS HERSELF OFF AND TRIES AGAIN.**

That's the beauty of how to be a good mom. She keeps trying to be the best she can be. A good mother is selfless yet recognizes that she needs "her own time" to care for her family. Good moms teach their children right from wrong, even when it is hard. They are there for their kids when they need them most, but they also know how to let them soar on their own when ready. And when they fail, good moms help them, dust them off, and encourage them to keep trying!

HOW TO BE A GOOD MOM

So, of course, there is the age-old question of how to be a good mom. What do we do to reach a good mom's status in life? It has been a worry capable of taking sleep from every woman's eye. But the tips below can be of help to every mother out there.

INNER CRITIC

Being a good mom means that you release your inner critic. No mother should ever compare herself to any other parent. Like children, no two mothers are alike, and each parenting style has its place. So as we release our inner critic, we start feeling we are doing a good job and belong in the good moms club.

YOUR BEST IS GOOD ENOUGH

We all strive to do our best, but the problem begins when we feel our best isn't good enough. No matter what we do, we might feel that our efforts are inadequate, but stop and think for a minute about how

> **KIDS WON'T REMEMBER WHAT THEY HAD, BUT THEY WILL REMEMBER THE MEMORIES YOU CREATED TOGETHER.**

your son or daughter sees it, especially while they're young. Kids won't remember what they had, but they will remember the memories you created together.

TAKE BETTER CARE OF YOURSELF

Self-care is an important part of being a good mother. A mom who doesn't care for herself cannot care for her children. A mother who never takes time out for herself will feel stressed and unloved. She cannot love others when stressed and unloved, especially her children.

So practice taking some time out for yourself often. Read a book, soak in the tub, exercise, and get a pedicure. Whatever it is that will make you feel better and come back refreshed, do that so you can keep being a good mom.

LESS IS MORE

Children, especially when they are young, enjoy the simple things in life. Kids may not remember the elaborate lengths you went through to throw them the perfect birthday party, the big pile of presents they received.

A child's focus is scattered onto so many things all at once, but these small moments you create will shine a bright light on your child's memories.

COMMUNICATION IS THE KEY

Communication is key when figuring out how to be a good mom. Regardless of how much your child does or doesn't talk to you, communication is about much more than the number of words that come from your child's

> **NO MATTER HOW BUSY YOU ARE, ESTABLISH GOOD COMMUNICATION EARLY WITH YOUR KIDS SO THAT WHEN PARENTING THEM GETS MORE COMPLICATED, YOU HAVE YEARS OF PRACTICE OF COMMUNICATING WITH THEM.**

mouth. No matter how busy you are, establish good communication early with your kids so that when parenting them gets more complicated, you have years of practice of communicating with them.

DATE YOUR KIDS INDIVIDUALLY

Funny right? Every child needs to feel important, and one of the best ways to make your children important is to spend time with each of them individually.

Sure, family time is important, but make sure that you have some time set aside for each child, and use this time to communicate and learn about their interests.

> **ONE OF THE BEST WAYS TO MAKE YOUR CHILDREN IMPORTANT IS TO SPEND TIME WITH EACH OF THEM INDIVIDUALLY.**

SET REASONABLE EXPECTATIONS

You can't expect the house to be spotless when little ones run around. Just like when you have teenagers, you can't expect them to tell you everything happening in their life down to the smallest detail.

DO LESS WELL

Many times we push to be wonder-working mothers. We wish to have a spotless house all the time, help our kids with their homework, research, and deliver a presentation that wows our clients over the dinner hour, and still have a hot, homemade meal on the dinner table at home. Of course, it's pretty hard to do all this simultaneously, so choose one thing you can focus on and do it well.

MAKE SURE THE DISCIPLINE MATCHES THE CRIME

Kids are bound to need discipline in their lives. Good moms take each situation and assign a punishment based on the crime. If kids are old enough, let them be punished reasonably. If the child is too young to understand this, make sure the punishment directly relates to what she did. This is important because many children receiving punishments tend to calculate the love of their parents with the punishment. For instance, if Ada is punished for taking the biscuit without permission, she expects that when Obi does the same, he should be punished and not ignored.

ALLOW YOUR KIDS TO FAIL

No parent should ever run around behind their child, fixing all of their mistakes. Of course, it's important to be there if your child makes a big mistake and to make sure he knows he can turn to you, but allowing them to take responsibility for their actions is vital in teaching them to live independent lives, learning from their mistakes.

> **ALLOWING YOUR CHILDREN TO TAKE RESPONSIBILITY FOR THEIR ACTIONS IS VITAL IN TEACHING THEM TO LIVE INDEPENDENT LIVE, LEARNING FROM THEIR MISTAKES.**

Remember, being a good enough mom isn't a matter of perspective. It's a fact that you are already good enough. You only have to believe that you are.

HOW TO WIN THE BATTLE CAUSED BY YOURSELF

Lack of care for yourself is a battle many women fight in their homes. Most of them go through other struggles and try to tackle the fight without knowing that the lack of taking care of themselves is the cause of the second problem.

For instance, a dirty woman might have a genuine reason for being busy with house chores that, most times, she forgets to take her bath. Now this might result in the husband distancing himself from her. He might be unable to explain his reasons to her, but it is becoming a serious problem.

These tips and ideas are simple ways to nourish yourself so that you can be the mom your kids need and the wife your husband desires.

EXERCISE
Do your favourite exercises always. It doesn't mean you have to run 5 miles a day. You can do stretching, yoga, or walking – the point is to get your body moving.

TAKE A BATH
There is a sweet secret pleasure in taking one's bath. Getting a bath is great, but having it benefits you more. Use homemade bath salts and quality essential oils for detox and relaxation.

TAKE A NAP
This is another great idea that, when implemented, can help you relax and ease stress. Taking a break and resting your body on the couch for some minutes can

make a difference in your perception of the day and how much energy you have until bedtime!

SAYING NO

Sometimes there are things on your to-do list that are not critical to your family's life. Eliminating the unessential responsibilities off your list will not only create some extra time and space but also lighten the burden you're feeling to keep up with it.

Feeling overwhelmed will quickly put any mom into orbit.

GET SLEEP

It is undoubtedly wisdom to sleep. Sleep is essential for you to stay healthy and be at your best.

GET CREATIVE

Do something that engages your creative side. Find some time to fit in a hobby that you enjoy!

KEEP CONNECTED

Friendships are important, and when our busy schedules get overloaded, those times of chatting or having coffee with friends dwindle. Isolation can quickly creep in, which is not where God wants us to be. Make sure you are purposeful in engaging and relationship-building.

WRITE A DAILY GRATITUDE LIST

A daily gratitude list is beneficial to shift your focus and help you appreciate any situation. It doesn't have to be long.

A few sentences will do, or just a list. If you keep a gratitude journal, you can reflect on your previous entries whenever you need a little boost of happiness and motivation.

LIMIT YOUR MEDIA CONSUMPTION

Yep, cut it out. If you stay more on social media, you will be prone to see things that seem real when they aren't. You may be tempted to imitate a lifestyle that won't work for you.

HAVE TIME ALONE

Get at least 30 minutes off your time each day and be by yourself. This time could be during your lunch break, before bed, or in the morning before everyone else gets up.

MAKE HEALTHIER CHOICES

Make better choices about your food – less sugar, more fresh fruits and vegetables, and ditch the soda. Your body will reward you when you take the time to make good choices rather than making decisions out of convenience or time restraints.

MEDITATE ON SCRIPTURE

Each week pick a Scripture to focus on – you don't necessarily need to memorize it, but write it out on a card and place it in a place you will surely see several times during the day.

ALWAYS PRAY

Needless to say, this probably should be at the top of the list. We often get into dilemmas and try to get out of them rather than going to the ONE who can perform miracles. Make it a practice to pray throughout your day, not just at certain times.

CHAPTER FIVE

SOCIETY TODAY

Building a healthy family should be the target of every woman because the family has a remarkable impact on society. The primary function of the family is to ensure the continuation of society, both biologically through procreation and socially through socialization. Given these functions, the nature of one's role in the family changes over time. From the children's perspective, the family instills a sense of orientation: it functions to locate children socially and plays a significant role in their socialization.

From the point of view of the parents, the family's primary purpose is procreation. The family functions to produce and socialize children. In some cultures, marriage imposes upon women the obligation to bear children. In northern Ghana, for example, payment of bridewealth signifies a woman's requirement to bear children, and women using birth control face substantial threats of physical abuse and reprisals.

IS FAMILY A SOCIETY?

The modern family structure can be considered an individual society in itself. The nuclear family has a distinct set of rules and values that apply to their family lives that may not apply to other family types or people in society. For example, single-parent families who have independent family structures may bond over their similarities and come together to create a support network for other single-parent families.

THE IMPORTANCE OF A HEALTHY FAMILY TO THE SOCIETY

Life has changed so much for most of us in the modern world. With the advancement of technology, changing cultural norms, new priorities, and new forms of communication fueled by the internet, it's natural to wonder what the importance of the family is. Is it a dying institution that has no place in modern life?

Well, of course not. Family is just as relevant as it ever was, if not more. No matter how much life changes in the future, it will probably continue to be needed in one form or another.

> **FAMILY IS JUST AS RELEVANT AS IT WAS, IF NOT MORE.**

The benefits of being in a healthy family have increased. As modern life puts pressure on all of us, the benefits of living in a family are more important than ever. Here is a list of some of the benefits.

HELPS MEET BASIC NEEDS

The basic social unit called the family is tasked with meeting the basic needs of those family members who can't provide for themselves. These include minors, the elderly and disabled, or those who can't afford to live alone. Basic needs such as food, water, shelter, and clean air are accessible when one or more members can provide these things for the whole family.

ALLOWS YOU TO BELONG TO SOMETHING

Many years ago, Abram Maslow created a diagram called the 'Hierarchy of Needs.' This hierarchy showed which needs were most crucial to humans. The broad base of Maslow's pyramid diagram represented the basic needs mentioned above, which must be met first. The security needs are on the next level up, followed by the love and belonging needs. Families spend so much time and energy supporting each other through difficult times because of the bonds they've created and nurtured since they became a part of the family.

FINANCIAL SECURITY

A well-functioning family provides financial security for everyone living in the household. First, family members who can work contribute at least a part of their earnings to help the family meet everyone's needs and wants. Second, the family combines resources to pay bills and manage their money to ensure that financial necessities are always taken care of.

BUILT-IN SUPPORT SYSTEM

Many people have found themselves with great news but no one to tell it to. That's a problem one rarely has when living in a family. People in healthy families have access to everyday joys that some don't. A healthy family has each other's back. When family members are stressed, someone close to them will most likely see the symptoms they're struggling with. People may hide their problems from others, but their family most often already understands. Even if they don't condone someone's actions, they love unconditionally. They're there for family members.

MY ADVICE TO ALL WOMEN IN FIGHTING SILENT BATTLES IN THEIR MARRIAGE

"More marriages might survive if the partners realized that sometimes the better comes after, the worse." I am sure that no marriage was planned from the outset to fail and have the woman suffer unless, for a few, where the husband intentionally marries a woman to punish her or her family, etc.

Hard times and conflicts are inevitable in any marriage –they're just a part of life. Whether the conflicts be internal (disagreement or stalemate, infidelity, health crises, mental illness, early marriage/child bride, etc.) or external conflicts (loss, tragedy, job stress or loss, family or in-law issues, etc.), you're going to face a mixture of them throughout your marriage. The trick is knowing how to stick together through them all.

> **STICK TOGETHER WITH YOUR HUSBAND THROUGH HARD TIMES AND CONFLICTS, WHICH ARE INEVITABLE IN ANY MARRIAGE. YOU WILL COME OUT VICTORIOUS.**

REMEMBER, YOU'RE TEAMMATES

Difficulties in your life can throw your entire marriage off kilter. While each situation must be assessed and approached uniquely, the good overarching idea is to remember that you're in the same team; you aren't enemies. When you function as teammates, tackling life's problems together is easier–and less likely that you'll turn on one another. Here are some tips for sticking together:

- Face your conflict head-on together; don't bury or avoid it! Don't assassinate one another's character or belittle each other.

- Communicate openly about what you're going through, and listen to one another. Be present for each other; no checking out allowed.

- If you're finding it increasingly difficult to work together as partners through this season, consider getting outside, objective help from a trusted counselor or pastor. This can help you focus on your primary objective: sticking together and coming out of this stronger.

CULTIVATE INTIMACY

Every relationship has seasons; love has its natural ebb and flow. But it's almost guaranteed that most marriages will experience dry spells amid challenging times. Tough situations are very consuming, which can drain all your energy before you can give your marriage the attention it needs. At some point in most marriages, it's typical for spouses to say, "We were soul mates, but now we're roommates." When you've been dealing with difficult issues, you might come out of it feeling like this.

If you've managed to hold onto each other and get through your unique situation together, you're one step ahead of the pack already. Clearly, your commitment to each other is still there–but it has been tested, and it might feel pretty empty emotionally.

Just because your relationship isn't fulfilling this season doesn't mean it's dead. It just needs to be revived. You're not going to feel emotionally connected to each other 100% of the time, and that's just how life is. The trick is getting connected again, and you can do this by cultivating intimacy.

To ignite more intimacy in your marriage:

- Revisit things you have in common.
- Reminisce together.
- Invest in the interests or activities that excite your spouse.
- Laugh together!

We can't emphasize this enough. Laughing together will help you revive the connection you've been lacking. Tough times can take a lot out of you, including simple things like laughter. Bring that back to life, and you'll be amazed at what it does for your marriage.

TAKE ONE DAY AT A TIME

Hard seasons in marriage make time feel like it's dragging by. We know how hard it is to wait for a particular season to pass. Grief, heartbreak, job loss, disconnection, illness, and similar issues all have to run their course, and sometimes it feels like the pain will never end. Just take one day at a time, keep holding onto one another, and you'll come out on the other side stronger than ever.

Most importantly, you need to talk to someone when facing challenging moments in your marriage. My sister's situation worsened, even to death, because she didn't speak out or trust anyone to share her experience.

As much as trusting people these days is difficult, it remains the best way to start your healing process. You can visit a therapist, your spiritual covers, or anyone you highly esteem.

Don't bottle up your grieves because you are trying to protect a marriage that may end up causing your death.

> **DON'T BOTTLE UP YOUR GRIEVANCES BECAUSE YOU ARE TRYING TO PROTECT A MARRIAGE THAT MAY END UP CAUSING YOUR DEATH.**

OTHER BOOKS BY THE AUTHOR

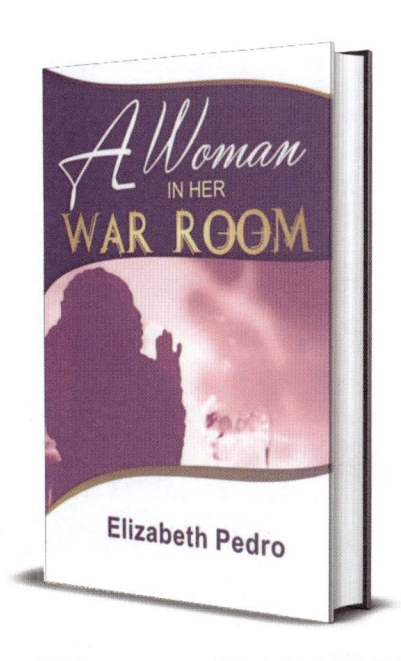

A Woman In Her War Room is an eye-opening series which is aimed at revealing what women go through in their lives as girls, young ladies, or adults, and how they can win this war in their war room. The different volumes of this book series will be revealing the kinds of wars women fight and the testimonies of people who have been through bad situations as women, and how they won through preparations in their war rooms. This is the first volume in the series: a must-read, not just for women, but also for men, so that they too will understand the wars fought by women, prepare themselves by the grace of God to help in one way or the other for a victorious outcome, for the benefit of society and to God's glory.

WOMEN EMPOWERMENT CONFERENCE PICTURES

WOMEN EMPOWERMENT CONFERENCE PICTURES

WOMEN EMPOWERMENT CONFERENCE PICTURES

AUTHOR'S BIOGRAPHY

Apostle Dr. Elizabeth Pedro (CGPA) is a transformation coach and mentor who believes every woman is a celebrity. As such, she supports, informs, and advocates for women and girls on the issues that affect them. She is a prolific writer, a motivational singer, and a global speaker who has been featured in high-impact events. She has spoken on stages across Five Continents and over 15 countries. She is passionate about Human

Capacity Development and loves talking humorously, using real-life stories to captivate her audience.

Dr. Liz is a certified marriage and relationship coach with the Institute of Marriage and Family Affairs TIMFA USA and the CEO of Serenity Coaching/Counselling Services.
Master Coach Practitioner (Online), Ontario Colleges.
Registered Practical Nurse Diploma, Seneca College, Toronto, Canada.
Diploma in Theology Canadian Christen Ministries (CCM) Toronto, Canada
Bachelor's degree in Theology Benson Idahosa University Nigeria.
Master's Degree in Theology and a Doctor's in Ministry, CICA University USA.
Dr. Liz has been featured in several media, including CBC Edmonton Canada and ITV Nigeria. In 2021 she was listed among the 50 most influential women in Edo state, Nigeria.

Dr. Liz is a philanthropist, and through her organization (WHW), she continues to impact women in her community and across the globe with skills acquisitions and stipends to start businesses on various skills learned with a vision to support the Sustainable

Development Goals-5, Achieve Gender Equality and empower all women and girls.

She is the founder/CEO of Agape For All Nations Int'l (Afani) and Women Helping Women For A Sustainable Tomorrow, NGOs focused on supporting and empowering women to become the best version of themselves. Her mission is to help women discover their unique selves by bringing hope through empowerment.

Her favourite quote is, "Empower a woman; you empower a nation."

Dr. Elizabeth Pedro is a recipient of over 25 Awards in different categories and several nominations, which include:
- Ambassador of Hope.
- Award of Excellency.
- Religious & Humanitarian Award.
- Presidential Lifetime Achievement Award.
- Generation Equality Naomi Award.
- Volunteer Viguor Award.
- Award Of Commander Of The Most Noble Order Of Peace Ambassador (CGPA).

Her Excellency Dr. Elizabeth Pedro is a peace ambassador to the UN, certified marriage mentor, a

Marriage and Relationship Coach, and the CEO of Serenity Coaching, a consulting outfit focused on training and consulting services on marriage, relationships, and family life issues.

She is also the award-winning author of the book "Woman in Her War Room" which has become a companion and guide to women around the globe.

Apostle Dr. Elizabeth is the co-founder of Great Shepherd Ministries (GSM) Edmonton. She is an ordained minister of the Gospel of Jesus with the Eagle Worldwide Ministries and Canadian Christian Ministries. (CCM). She is the President of School of Chaplain, Alberta Region of Canada.

Dr. Liz is married to the love of her life, and they are blessed with two (2) boys.

NOTES